YOUR RIGHT TO HEAVEN

DONALD G. BARNHOUSE

D1527214

BAKER BOOK HOUSE
Grand Rapids, Michigan

Foreword

The year was 1953, the place was Tampa, Florida. I was the manager of an Arthur Murray Dance Studio in that city. After having been out most of the night at a party, I was awakened by my alarm clock radio about two in the afternoon. The voice that roused me from my sleep was obviously the voice of a preacher. Since I did not bother to go to church I felt no need for a preacher—especially in my bedroom and most especially when I had a hangover. I reached over to change the dial but was stopped by the penetrating question by Dr. Barnhouse: "What answer would you give if death had just claimed you and God would say to you, 'What right have you to come into My heaven?'" I was stunned! I had never considered such a matter before in my life. I just sat with my mouth open on the edge of the bed and heard the gospel for the first time in my life. I was stunned and incredulous, but six days later, as a result of that question and that message, the Lord brought me to Himself.

Sometime thereafter He called me into the ministry of the Word. While I was in seminary in Atlanta, Dr. Barnhouse gave a series of messages at one of the local churches. That was the first and last meeting that I ever had with him but I had the pleasure, at his request, of sharing this testimony with the congregation gathered there that night.

After entering the pastorate, God slowly led in the development of a program of training laymen for evangelism. It is known as Evangelism Explosion International, and it is now found in almost fifty nations of the world. The program still centers around a slightly modified form of the diagnostic question which Dr. Barnhouse used so effectively with me.

Through his broad radio and preaching ministry he reached tens of thousands of people. I'm only sorry that he did not live long enough to see the indirect results of his efforts in the Evangelism Explosion ministry throughout the world.

This will be an excellent book to place in the hands of non-Christians to confront them squarely and plainly with the gospel of Jesus Christ. It would also help new Christians to more fully understand the meaning of the gospel and the Christian walk.

May God grant that this new edition of *Your Right to Heaven* may continue as good seed to produce a great harvest for our Savior.

D. JAMES KENNEDY
President, Evangelism Explosion International
Pastor, Coral Ridge Presbyterian Church

Contents

1
What Do You Want Out of Life?

What is the most sought-after thing in the world? Is it money? A man says he will be happy if he can get a thousand dollars saved up. He gets his thousand, and then says that he would like to have five thousand. He gets the five thousand and wants ten. He gets the ten and wants fifty. He reaches that goal and starts for the hundred thousand. When he counts his fortune at that figure he thinks of half a million. As soon as he has reached that, he dreams of his million. The more he gets, the more he wants. Even after he has accumulated more money than he or his family can possibly spend, he still continues to amass his fortune. The frenzied efforts that he makes prove that he is not really seeking after money, but after something else, an intangible something; the possession of money has not brought him what he has been seeking.

Someone else may think that the most sought-after thing in the world is power. But this is not true. Elect a man sheriff, and he will think of the state legislature. Elect him to the legislature, and he will want to be congressman. If he reaches Washington, he will want to go back as senator. Let him attain the Senate, and he will think in terms of the presidency. Power alone does not satisfy. Napoleon himself once said, "What a bore life is! What a cross!" This proves that it is not the mere place of power that a man is seeking, but something else which he believes his success and power will bring him.

You may run on through the gamut of human efforts and human attainments, and it will always be the same story. The possession of education, fame, power, wealth, or success does not bring those who have reached their goals what they have really sought for. The proof lies in the many suicides among the successful, and the fact that wealthy and powerful men keep on running after they have "arrived."

Robert Burns wrote in his "Epistle to Davie":

> If happiness have not her seat
> And center in the breast,
> We may be wise, or rich or great,
> But never can be blest.

Even the founding fathers did not guarantee to our citizens the rights of life, liberty and happiness, but only the rights of life, liberty and the *pursuit* of happiness.

What men are really seeking is something that can never be found by man, for what they seek is peace with God. This is the thing most sought after in the world. The apostle Paul tells us in Romans 5:1—"Therefore, being justified by faith, we have peace with God through our Lord Jesus Christ." By implication this means that man cannot reach the goal of peace by his own efforts.

One of the many names of God is "the God of peace," and if we understand this characteristic of His nature, we will have laid the groundwork for the possession of peace in our own hearts. But first, let us ask ourselves if we know the meaning of the word *peace*. Perhaps this is one of those terms which we use often and assume we know, but when we're asked to give a proper definition, we find that we do not fully comprehend all that is involved in the term. The Oxford English Dictionary gives fifteen different definitions of the word *peace* in its noun form. If we look closely at some of these, we may have a better idea of what God is talking about in our text. And, perhaps some may learn why they are so restless in their own spirits.

The first definition of the word *peace* describes the relationship between nations. Peace is "freedom from, or cessation of, war or hostilities; that condition of a nation or community in which it is not at war with another." Another definition concerns individuals: "Freedom from disturbance or perturbation (especially as a condition in which an individual is); quiet, tranquility, undisturbed state. Emphasized as peace and quiet, or peace and quietness." Still another definition concerns the inward man: "Freedom from mental or spiritual disturbance or conflict arising from passion, sense of guilt, etc; calmness." We use this meaning in such phrases as "peace of mind, of soul, of conscience." Finally, and most important, the dictionary states: "In general, [peace is] the sense including several of the above." Under this heading, our dictionary quotes certain passages from the Bible and speaks of the peace of God as an illustration.

In order to understand the peace that God gives, let us reexamine the first definition, which

9

concerns the relationship between two countries. Peace is "freedom from, or cessation of, war or hostilities." This applies to the spiritual realm as well. Every soul has been at war with God; in order for reconciliation to take place, there must be a cessation of the warfare, the hostilities, which exist between the individual and the Creator. The question that must be answered, therefore, is: How is the warfare that exists between the soul and God to come to an end?

The first part of the answer is that we must realize that the war exists and confess the fact. A man who tries to insist that there is nothing wrong between him and God is dodging the truth. There is warfare between every man and God by the very nature of man's sinful heart. God says that the warfare exists, and we have to admit it. In Romans 8:5-8, Paul expresses the matter with finality: "For they that are after the flesh do mind the things of the flesh; but they that are after the Spirit the things of the Spirit. For to be carnally minded is death; but to be spiritually minded is life and peace. Because the carnal mind is enmity against God, for it is not subject to the law of God, neither indeed can be." Phillips translates these verses: "The carnal attitude sees no further than natural things; but the spiritual attitude reaches out after the things of the Spirit. The former attitude means, bluntly, death; but the latter means life and inward peace. And this is only to be expected for the carnal attitude is inevitably opposed to the purpose of God, and neither can nor will follow His laws for living. Men who hold this attitude cannot possibly please God."

The fact that the natural heart of man is hostile toward God must, because of God's holiness and His justice, call forth wrath from Him toward the individual. We are "by nature the children of wrath" (Eph. 2:3). After we admit that man is at war with God, we must then ask: How can this state of things come to an end?

Let us examine how a war between two nations comes to an end. A French statesman once pointed out that there were only two types of peace that ever followed a war: A peace imposed upon the defeated by a conqueror; or a peace accepted by the defeated through surrender. There is a vast difference between the peace which is imposed or the peace which one accepts.

It should be evident that if there is to be peace between a human being and God, the terms must be imposed by God Himself. God, the eternal God, the Supreme Being, must have His way—it is the only right way in the universe. Every other way is the way of the creature, the way of earth. Men who will not submit their wills to the Creator go their horrible way to a Christless eternity.

Yet in spite of the fact that our position and our condition are defenseless, there have been those who have talked about "making their peace with God," as if *they* had a right to set the terms. The phrase has long been in use to describe settling differences between *men*. Shakespeare, in *Twelfth Night*, has one of his characters say: "I will make your peace with him, if I can." Thomas Fuller seems to have been the first man who ever spoke of making one's peace with

God. But the phrase is incorrect in such a connection, though many have thus used it.

If you are to know the joys of what God has
for you, you must get that idea out of your
mind. You must realize that God has already
made the peace and that you are to simply
accept it. And when you come to God, the
wonderful thing is that you find Him merciful
toward you. The soul who flings himself upon
the promises of God finds that the Creator is the
loving Savior. God has already made peace and is
ready to receive that soul with all grace and
tenderness. In the epistle to the Colossians, we
read of the Lord Jesus Christ that "it pleased the
Father that in him should all fulness dwell; And,
having made peace through the blood of his
cross, by him to reconcile all things unto himself. . ." (Col. 1:19, 20). Note especially the
tense of the verb: Having made peace.

This is of paramount importance: God *has
made* peace. There is no other peace that can be
made except that which God has made. A man
who talks about making his peace with God
denies the peace which God has already made.
God will have no other peace with man than
that which He has made at the cross. If a man
refuses the peace which God has provided
through the Lord Jesus Christ at the cross, then
he remains at enmity with God (see John
3:17-18: *already lost!*). The hostility of his soul
is still evident, and he must carry into all eternity the fruits of the holy wrath of God. This
wrath must break forth against those who "hath
trodden under foot the Son of God, and hath
counted the blood of the covenant, wherewith
he was sanctified, an unholy thing, and hath

done despite unto the Spirit of grace" (Heb. 10:29).

But, if you will come with an absolute capitulation and unconditional surrender, you will find that God is all peace toward you. It is then that you can go on to find that second rest which God provides for those who surrender to Himself.

Peace with God is an accomplished fact, but it is ours only when we are justified by faith. This points once more to the cross of Jesus Christ. There, traced in characters of blood, are the requirements which God imposes on the soul that will approach Him. Those of us who have come to the cross know that we have peace with God. We know that there is nothing which He can hold against the one who has thus been justified (Rom. 8:1).

There are multitudes who testify of this same peace with God. The major lines of the testimony are always the same. I can give it in terms of my own experience. I was a sinner, which means that I was less perfect than God. By the conviction of the Holy Spirit, I came to know that my state of imperfection would incur the condemnation of God if I did not submit myself to His grace. I acknowledged before Him that I was a sinner and threw myself on His mercy and grace. I recognized that he had taken all the steps toward me, and that He had made salvation possible through Jesus Christ, His Son. When God the Father put God the Son to death on the cross, He provided the way by which He could proclaim the manifesto of His grace and pardon to all who would submit to Him or, to put it in John's words, "receive Him" (John 1:11, 12).

Though I know myself to be a sinner, I have no concern whatsoever about the penalty of sin, since the Lord Jesus Christ bore the penalty and declared me righteous.

It is this love, and all that flows from it, which becomes the constraining factor in my life as I seek to glorify Him as Lord. I know Him as my Creator and have peace of mind. I know Him as Savior and have peace of conscience. And in the measure that I enter into the second rest, I know Him as Lord and so find the peace that passes all understanding (Phil. 4:7). These ideas are developed through all the Word of God, and through all the life of the believer.

2
How Tall
Are You?

The quality of height is greatly admired. Tourist folders from the western U.S. speak of the great peaks of the Rockies. Great cities speak of their skyscrapers—New York takes pride in its Empire State Building, a mid-western city boasts the tallest granary building in the country, and so Texas is forced to gloat about its tall tales.

When it comes to people we still find height an admirable quality. Short people desire to be tall. Tall people desire to have tall people as their mates. In fact, one shoe company advertised, "With our shoes, now you can be taller than she is." There is a certain psychological bent in man's very nature that demands him to be tall. If a man is not physically tall, he tries to make up for it mentally, by egotism, or with a domineering spirit.

Men cannot stand to be inferior, to be in the lesser position. They want to feel equal with all men, and find it difficult to admit that other men are superior to them. In Romans 3:23 the apostle Paul writes, "For all have sinned and come short of the glory of God." This interesting phrase, "come short," brings to mind the quality of tallness. How tall is God? How short are we? How far short of His standards do we fall? What is the distance of our come-shortness?

After the first world war there were tens of thousands of American soldiers who were left in France, and their supreme desire was to get home as rapidly as possible. Discipline was greatly relaxed from the tension of wartime, and the men were securing as much leave as possible in order to see the sights of Europe. In a certain village about a hundred miles from Paris there was a detachment of American soldiers—a lieutenant and about forty men—who were guarding an ammunition dump. There was little to do outside of the brief periods of guard duty, but the men amused themselves as best they could.

One day, while the lieutenant was on leave, a motorcycle messenger came from General Pershing's headquarters. He brought word that 2,700 men were to be chosen to march in the peace parades of London, Paris, Brussels, and Rome. The corporal and sergeant who read the order discovered that there were two conditions imposed as standards for selection. The first brought them no difficulty, for it stated that every candidate had to have a clean record—no man would be chosen who had been court-martialed. But the second condition made them pause. The order stated that every man applying had to be at least one meter and eighty-six centimeters tall.

The corporal looked at the sergeant and the sergeant looked at the corporal and asked him how much one meter and eighty-six centimeters was. There was no answer. Then the corporal said the most natural thing under the circumstances: "At any rate, Sarge, I am taller than you."

When the news spread around the group, it was the same thing over again. No one knew the metric system. The men got into arguments about their relative heights, and soon they were standing up, back to back, to see who was the tallest man in the company. Finally, they knew their comparative heights, all the way from Slim down to Shorty. Slim was very proud and told them that he would send them a postcard from Rome and that he would take a look at the English girls for the rest of them. Poor Shorty received the good-natured banter of his fellows.

Under the circumstances, these soldiers did the normal, natural thing. They were in ignorance of the required standard. The information was greatly desired. This led them to set up artificial standards of their own and measure themselves by themselves. Some pride developed in the men who were taller. After all, were they not the most probable candidates?

Then the officer returned. He read the order and asked if there were any candidates. "The trouble is, sir," the sergeant replied, "we do not know what one meter and eighty-six centimeters is." The lieutenant, who knew French, went to the village and brought back a meter measure. Soon a mark was made on the wall of the required height (about six feet). Now the men were no longer measuring themselves with themselves. They had to stand up against a mark on the wall that was inflexible. It had been established by General Pershing. One or two men backed up to the mark, and their companions told them that they were an inch or so short of the mark. Some men merely looked at the mark and knew that there was no hope. Finally, a call was made for Slim, and he came to be measured. He pulled himself up to his greatest possible height and stood there, rigid and puffed up, as they measured him. He, too, was short, even though he was short by no more than a quarter of an inch.

Of course, General Pershing got his 2,700 men. Many saw them that day when they came under the Arch of Triumph on Bastille Day, the fourteenth of July. These men, all in new uniforms, and with American Beauty roses tied to their bayonets, made a proud sight as they marched down the Champs Elysees, each one of them at least one meter and eighty-six centimeters tall!

The point of my story lies in the fact that Pershing did not secure *any* of his marching men from the company I have described. He was not asking that they be *about* so tall, but that they fill an *absolute* requirement. And the heart of my story lies in the fact that tall Slim did not march in the parade any more than did short Shorty.

As General Pershing had a perfect right to set the standard which determined the height of every man that was in that parade, so it is with God. The apostle Paul says in Romans 3:22, 23: "For there is no difference: for all have sinned and come short of the glory of God." Now God's standard, therefore, is His glory. This standard must be met, and since it is God's Heaven to which we wish to go, He has the right to set the standards for entrance therein. He has the right to make His own rules, even as we human beings make the rules for entry into our houses. You do not go to a man's house in the middle of the night and seek to enter surreptitiously by a ladder through a second story window. If you go to a man's house, you go to the front door and ring the bell or knock on the door or make some other noise signifying your presence. And the Lord God has as much right to make the rules for entry into His home, Heaven, as you do for entry into your house.

The rule which God has made for entry into Heaven is: Men shall measure up to His glory and be as perfect as He is. This rigorous standard is to be found expressed throughout the Bible, and it is to be found exemplified in the man Christ Jesus. The Old Testament was built around the command of God, "Ye shall be holy, for I am holy" (Lev. 11:44).

God has demanded absolute perfection as the prerequisite for entry into Heaven. This is quite reasonable, for if He should demand anything less, Heaven would become filled with men who were imperfect. It would never more be Heaven, but merely earth moved to Heaven. Stop and think of your own case. If you were taken into Heaven exactly as you are at this present moment, without any change whatsoever, you would befoul Heaven. Heaven would no longer be pure and holy, as it must be in order to be a fit dwelling place for the Holy God.

Like the soldiers in my story, when the law was given to men, they did not understand the meaning of the terms. "Be ye holy" meant no more to them than one meter eighty-six centimeters meant to the soldiers in the village. So, men did the most natural thing in the world.

They began measuring themselves among themselves. Little by little the human race adopted various standards which classify human beings. They did not judge themselves according to their physical statures, as Slim and Shorty, but according to various other standards. Some men are so foolish as to measure by the pigmentation of their skins. There have been those who have thought that intrinsic worth had something to do with whether a man was white or dark-skinned. Any sensible man knows, immediately, that there are going to be white men in Hell as well as in Heaven, and there are going to be black men in Heaven as well as in Hell:

It makes no difference whether the flesh
    Be black, or white, or brown,
The dying Saviour wore for all
    The thorny crown.

Others have measured themselves according to their culture, or the accomplishment of certain rites or ceremonies, or their educational attainment. All of this is as futile as the measuring of the soldiers in the French mess hall. How just would God be if He based salvation on something that man could do? That would mean that some people would be totally incapable of fulfilling the requirements and others would have a natural advantage that would give them a head start.

In the case of the soldiers, Pershing found tall men in other camps. But there are *none* who can fulfill God's standards. All have sinned and are falling short of the glory of God. He put up His standard of measurement, and declared that the whole race falls short of His standard. That standard of measurement is found in God's law, and it is also embodied in the Savior, the Lord Jesus Christ. But either way you look at it, you and I and all other men have fallen short of the glory of God. If you measure yourself by the written law, you fall short; you have sinned. If you stand beside the Lord Jesus Christ, you are immediately dwarfed in comparison.

Suppose God had based entrance into Heaven on money. If the requirements were the possession of a hundred million dollars, then ninety-nine and a fraction percent of all men would be condemned to Hell. They would have no possible hope of meeting the requirements. If God had based salvation on human intelligence, then Heaven would be peopled with a few Einsteins, Newtons, and similar minds, and the morons and ordinary people would be in Hell. Such standards would be totally unjust, because men often have very little control over their intelligence or financial status.

In the same way, if God had based salvation on human character, He would have been unjust. A man or woman fortunate enough to have been born in a home where godly parents gave the children the necessary lessons in character training would have an inestimable advantage over a poor unfortunate one born to parents who were permissive, unconcerned, or even dissolute.

But God Almighty does not work on any such unjust basis. He establishes His perfect standard, measures you by it, declares that you *fall short* and can never do anything to meet His requirements, and then proceeds, by the same method, to declare righteous the ungodly who believe in the Lord Jesus Christ.

No man should ever think that he gets any-
where near the standard that has been set by
God. In our story of the soldiers, Slim missed
the mark by only a quarter of an inch. The Lord
Jesus Christ says that men have fallen short of
God's mark by much more than this. In the
Sermon on the Mount, the Lord looked out over
the people and said, "Except your righteousness
shall exceed the righteousness of the scribes and
Pharisees, ye shall in no case enter into the kingdom of heaven" (Matt. 5:20). These men had
whittled down the law and had put spiritual
wedgies in their shoes and had said, "We pass,
We pass." The Lord says to the multitude: "It is
not so. They do not pass." And our Lord adds:
"Which of you by taking thought can add one
cubit unto his stature?" (Matt. 6:27). A cubit is
eighteen inches. The Lord tells men that they
are not merely a fraction of an inch short, but
that they are so short that it is impossible for a
man to provide the difference which is lacking.
No man can grow to the stature that will meet
God's moral requirements. And any man who
attempts to make stilts for himself to pass on
the day of measurement will discover that the
judgment of God is according to truth, and he
will surely be cut down. There is no escape. All
have sinned and are falling short of the glory of
God.

The verb which is here translated "come
short" is found many places in the New Testament and is translated by nine different English
words or phrases. These are: *come behind, come
short, be destitute, fail, lack, suffer need, want,
be in want,* and *be worse for.* Taken together,
these words show that our case is truly hopeless

apart from the intervening grace of God. No matter what our efforts, we are falling short of the glory of God.

If I took a group of people out into a field and told them to jump to the moon, some of them would not get more than six inches or a foot off the ground. The world's champion high jumper would be able to get about seven feet off the ground. With the use of a pole to vault, the champion pole vaulter could swing himself eighteen feet off the ground. But that is all. No man could reach the moon by his unaided efforts. And the man who gets eighteen feet off the ground is not much nearer the moon than the one who might be able to jump up six inches, or the invalid who cannot move at all. In the same way, all have sinned and all are falling short of the glory of God.

No man has ever made a gesture toward God that has reached God. That is why the Lord summarizes the commandments with the slaying word, "Thou shalt love the Lord thy God with all thy heart, and with all thy soul, and with all thy mind. . . . Thou shalt love thy neighbour as thyself" (Matt. 22:37, 39 and Deut. 6:5). What condemnation is here! What death! What a revelation of the failure of man! Have you ever had an emotion of the heart that was not for God? Then you are falling short of His glory. Have you ever had a thought of the mind that was not toward God? Then you are falling short of His glory. Have you ever loved yourself more than your neighbor? Then you are falling short of His glory.

Stop your efforts then, and rest in what He has done. His way is all-sufficient, and it alone satisfies God. Paul, in writing to the Corinthian church, said of God concerning our Lord Jesus Christ, "For he hath made him to be sin for us, who knew no sin; that we might be made the righteousness of God in him" (II Cor. 5:21). For this reason alone the Lord Jesus Christ went to the cross to take our sins and to make us righteous as God has required.

Yes, we can be as "tall" as God in the person of the Lord Jesus Christ. Today may you look away from yourself and your own inadequacies and look to the sufficiency of the cross, where the Lord Jesus died to make you like Himself. This is the true meaning of justification. Once the heart comes to appreciate this great truth, then there steals over it a peace not found on earth—it is a peace given from Heaven! Paul tells us, "Being justified by faith, we have peace with God through our Lord Jesus Christ" (Rom. 5:1).

3

Are You Camouflaged?

The first time I rode in an airplane I was immediately struck by the fact that the earth looked flatter from the air than from the ground. It was an old-fashioned airplane with open cockpits, and we looked over the side at the ground that was moving beneath us. We were not moving; we were the one still place in our universe, and the earth slipped beneath our wings with tremendous speed. We were moving more than a hundred miles an hour. And we were very high. We reached over two thousand feet on our first flight. We had risen from a cow pasture near Princeton where a group of us were beginning to learn how to fly planes; and when it came my turn to fly we went toward Trenton. I can still recapture some of the feeling of those moments. A ten-story building looked no higher than a one-story building. The earth was flat.

As aviators have pushed their machines higher and higher, this truth has become more evident. From fifty thousand feet above sea level, mountains become molehills and it is impossible to discern the smaller contours of the earth's surface. But you can come to the same conclusion without getting into a plane. Consider Mount Everest. It rises five miles above sea level on our planet, which is about eight thousand miles in diameter. Now consider a billiard ball two and a half inches in diameter. With a little figuring, you will discover that a bulge on the billiard ball proportionately as high as Mt. Everest, would be not a half inch or an eighth of an inch high, but less than one-six-hundredth of an inch high. Human fingers are not sensitive enough to even feel such a ridge on a billiard ball. If our earth were held in fingers no more sensitive than human fingers, it would feel perfectly smooth. However, when we live down in a valley or on one of the plains of our earth, we think of the mountains as being towering and majestic.

What is true of the earth geographically is also true of humanity spiritually. In the sight of God there are no moral differences between members of the human race. Some such differences seem large from our worm's-eye view, but when we rise to the eminence of the Biblical perspective and look down upon our earth, we see it is spiritually flat; all the efforts of humanity are seen to be vain imaginings.

The Bible says, "There is none righteous, no, not one: There is none that understandeth, there is none that seeketh after God. They are all gone out of the way, they are together become un-profitable; there is none that doeth good, no, not one. Their throat is an open sepulchre; with their tongues they have used deceit; the poison of asps is under their lips; whose mouth is full of cursing and bitterness: Their feet are swift to shed blood: Destruction and misery are in their ways: And the way of peace have they not known: There is no fear of God before their eyes" (Rom. 3:10-18). This paragraph in the third chapter of Romans views man from the divine perspective, and it is an appalling sight. Humanity lies before the Creator with all the human inequalities dismissed, and each member of the human race is seen as a part of the putrefying whole. No longer is there any consideration of men divided into religious or ethnic groups. They are seen as sons of Adam; and the sight is described in God's own vocabulary.

If we go back to the fourteenth Psalm, we find an introduction to these quotations: "The Lord looked down from heaven upon the children of men." The scene is described from the vantage point of God and the object of His gaze is the entire human race—you are definitely in the group. This, then, is the divine description of your heart by the nature of your birth.

We were born with the fallen nature of Adam. We are sinners by nature as we have remained sinners by choice. If any man were to be so foolish as to deny his guilt, the Creator-Judge has set forth this manifesto declaring what mankind really is in His sight. It is Light speaking, revealing the hidden things of darkness. It is Life speaking, analyzing the corruption of death. It is Righteousness speaking, declaring the evil of unrighteousness. It is definite, detailed, and final. There is not the faintest ray of hope left for the sinner apart from the one method which God is about to declare through Jesus Christ.

Most people live in a world where they have camouflaged the true circumstances of their lives in order to protect their old natures. They are not willing to accept the verdict which God has rendered concerning their own evil nature. The result is that they come to dwell, little by little, in a world of spiritual make-believe. If the old nature is to be delivered over to the Lord for crucifixion death, it must be recognized as existing and as being just what God says it is.

There is a human goodness (using the word in a limited sense) that shows how far man is fallen. An illustration will show what I mean. A spring comes forth from the side of a hill, clear, cold and pure. As the stream flows down through the countryside, it becomes polluted. By the time it reaches the sea it carries the filth of towns and cities. Yet there are traces of its original values that were present in it.

So is the goodness of mankind. Adam came fresh from the hand of God, and there was no sin within him. But he chose to follow his own will instead of remaining in creature submission to the will of God. So, there entered a death into the human stream which, under the analysis of the great Chemist, is seen in all its component parts in the paragraph from the book of Romans quoted above.

First of all, God declares that man's whole being is fallen. The Bible says that man has departed from God both actively and passively, and that he is foul in his motives and in his speech. Spoiled in himself, he has also spoiled his environment. The paragraph concludes by showing that all this horrible condition of man, individually and collectively, stems from the fact that he has turned his eyes away from God. He no longer acknowledges himself as a creature and God as his Creator.

We must not think that this passage is accusing every member of the human race of having committed all of these individual sins. It does teach that the roots of all sin are in all men. In some men the evil fruits lie dormant on some of their branches, but the awful potentialities are always present in the sap within the wood. Let me illustrate. When great bombs fell on London during World War Two and plowed up the earth to great depths, flowers sprang up from the earth. Many of these flowers had not been known within London for scores of years, and some had been lost to the botanist for more than a century. Do not consider yourself sinless, therefore, because you are not, in your overt actions, corrupt, deceitful, unloving, blasphemous, murderous, oppressive, and warlike. You may have all of these things grubbed down beneath the surface of the soil, but the roots are still there. They are there whether you want them or not. God says they are there.

This is why the indictment begins with the great charge: "There is none righteous; no, not one." It is interesting to note that the spelling of the word *righteous* has changed. Up until the sixteenth century, the word was written "right-wise," meaning "right way." Rightwise, or righteous, refers to "one who is such as he ought to be."

In the sight of God, only the Lord Jesus Christ is the beloved Son in whom He is well pleased. None other is righteous, for none is such as he ought to be. If you place yourself by Christ you will see that you are not righteous.

There is an old story about a woman who washed some fine linen and found it beautifully white. But when she placed it on the new-fallen snow it was yellowish in hue, revealing its intrinsic failure. So with the hearts of men. We will admit that there are men who are as white as fine linen, but Christ alone was white as snow. Are you less perfect than God? If you are, (and we all are) then you are unrighteous in His sight. You are in need of His salvation which He offers to you through His Son, the Savior.

The first effect of the unrighteousness of men is that "there is none that understandeth." Adam himself, immediately after the fall, manifested this lack of spiritual understanding by running away from the Creator God, to whom he should have turned. Ever since that moment, the higher nature of man—his spirit—has fallen into his soul as a third story of a building might fall into the second story of a bombed house. The debris of the two stories are mixed together, and the result is that a man may understand things of the world but he cannot understand the things of God; he cannot comprehend divine things. Anything that men have ever written about God based on any source apart from the divine revelation is not only a waste of time but is an affront to deity. That is why the entire philosophical literature about religion is a worthless heap.

The state of man is manifested further by the fact that not one man seeks after God or ever has sought after God. Do not look upon the horizons of the pagan cities, at the foul and obscene architecture of their temples and think that they are monuments to a search after God. I have been beneath those roofs and have seen there the signs of the most debased and perverted worship of the generative powers in nature. And do not think when you hear men talking about God apart from Christ that they are really seeking after God.

"Everybody talkin' 'bout Heaven ain't goin' there" says the Negro spiritual, and it is most certainly true. It is God who tells us that there is none that seeks after Him. Speaking of church membership, it has been well said that people go to church not to be saved but in order to be gentlemen. As you have read these lines, you may well ask yourself the question: "Why am I religious?" Is it really to know God? Or are you a member of a church in order that you may follow the custom of the times, simply because it is the thing to do? Why does God maintain that there is none that seek Him? Simply because to come to a knowledge of the Lord Jesus Christ means the total crucifixion of self, because the accepting of the Savior implies that the one who receives Him is lost, and this we do not want to admit.

Some time ago I read in a magazine a biography of Jesus Christ. It spoke of Christ the carpenter, of Christ the teacher, of Christ the working man, of Christ the social worker, of Christ the leader in great humanitarian movements. But not a word was spoken of Christ the Redeemer. The saving work of Christ—the very thing He came to earth for—was completely ignored. The reason for this was quite evident: the writer would not admit that he was a sinner. The natural man "receiveth not the things of the Spirit of God: for they are foolishness unto him: neither can he know [understand] them, because they are spiritually discerned" (I Cor. 2:14).

31

But, you may say, since this is the case, and yet I recognize what I have read to be true, what can I do? How may I come to know the Savior? How may I truly seek after God? There is one answer. Paul, who has given us this diagnosis of ourselves, ripping away the camouflage which we have put up, says "Faith cometh by hearing, and hearing by the word of God" (Rom. 10:17). Having seen what God has to say of our natural state, it is wonderful to know that He has also said that we are justified freely by His grace through the redemption that is in Christ Jesus (Rom. 3:24). God sent His Son to die on Calvary for every man, putting His righteousness to every man's account in order that God may see us through the righteousness of His dear Son who came to be our Savior.

In fact, this is the very message of the gospel. We read, "For God sent not his Son into the world to condemn the world; but that the world, through him [the Son] might be saved" (John 3:17). Will you not come to Him just as you are? Hear the Lord Jesus Himself speaking to you, "Verily, verily, I say unto you, He that heareth my word, and believeth on him that sent me, hath everlasting life, and shall not come into condemnation; but is passed from death unto life" (John 5:24).

No man who is imperfect in the least degree can ever enter God's holy Heaven. The standard is absolute, 100% perfection. Since no man can reach that standard, God sent His Son into the world to provide that standard for man. Thus it is through the merits of the Lord Jesus Christ and in His righteousness we can expect to see

God some day—not as our Judge, but as our Savior, for

> My hope is built on nothing less
> Than Jesus' blood and righteousness;
> I dare not trust the sweetest frame,
> But wholly lean on Jesus' name;
> On Christ, the solid Rock, I stand,
> All other ground is sinking sand.

4
The Dam of
God's Patience

The wrath of God is like the great waters im-
pounded behind a dam. I can remember the first
time I saw the great Hoover Dam. It has been
thrown across the waters of the Colorado River,
and these waters have backed up for scores of
miles, penetrating into every little cove and
valley. Thus it has been with the wrath of God.
The first time there was ever a sin committed,
the wrath of God was stored up against that sin.
As more men lived upon the earth, their hearts
grew more wicked and the outbreaks of their sin
more violent. And so, the store of wrath grew
greater and greater, held back by the patience of
God, which lies across the valley of His judgment like a great dam across the river. And in
His eternal foreknowledge, God the Father fore-
saw all our sin—and stored His wrath against it
behind the dam of His patience. And the wrath
of God against sin that even has not yet been
committed is all stored up, waiting for the day
when His patience shall come to its holy end.

What a thing to contemplate—the patience of
God. For thousands of years it held back His
wrath. Only occasionally in the course of history
did He stoop to dip His hand into the pent-up
flood and pour a few drops of wrath upon some

especially vicious outbreak of rebellion. But for the most part God seemed to overlook all of the sin of man in the centuries before the cross. It looked as though sin were condoned. Paul speaks of the fact that the "times of ignorance were winked at." This is a striking figure of speech that lights up the thought we are setting forth. The day of such apparent condoning is over. The cross is the revelation of the fact that God really means business with this question of sin, and woe to the man who thinks otherwise.

The Lord Jesus Christ came and stood before the dam of God's patience. There was placed the island of Calvary on which the cross was erected. When Christ was made sin for us, He became a curse, for we read in Galatians, "Cursed is every one that hangeth on a tree" (Gal. 3:13). In that dark hour the storm of God's wrath reached its peak. The sun grew dark, night fell upon the earth at noon. God broke down the dam of His patience and the raging waves of wrath flooded upon the Lord Jesus. All who ever had believed the Word of God about the shedding of the blood of the lamb in the Old Testament, and all who ever would believe in the death of the Lord Jesus in the ages since that day were seen to be standing on Calvary with Christ. When the dam broke the Lord Jesus died, but took the wrath of God against all those who have trusted in the Savior. It is no wonder that the Church breaks forth in song:

> Beneath the cross of Jesus
>   I fain would take my stand,
> The shadow of a mighty Rock
>   Within a weary land.

A home within the wilderness,
    A rest upon the way,
From the burning of the noontide heat,
    And the burden of the day.

Oh, safe and happy shelter!
    Oh, refuge tried and sweet!
Oh! trusting place where Heaven's love
    And Heaven's justice meet
As to the holy patriarch
    That wondrous dream was given
So seems my Saviour's cross to me
    A ladder up to heaven.

There lies beneath its shadow,
    But on the farther side
The darkness of an awful grave
    That gapes both deep and wide;
And there between us stands the cross,
    Two arms outstretched to save,
Like a watchman set to guard the way
    From that eternal grave.

And since God has done all this for us, since
there has been this prodigality of love in our
behalf, is it any wonder that He should reveal
His wrath against all ungodliness and unrighteousness of men? ("For the wrath of God is
revealed from heaven against all ungodliness and
unrighteousness of men, who hold the truth in
unrighteousness" Romans 1:18.) Why does the
Lord speak of these two qualities as evoking His
wrath? The words in the original language show
that they refer, in the one case, to acts against
God, and in the other, to acts against men. It is
strange to think of men committing acts against
God, and yet it is a fact, for we see that men

crucified Christ. When we realize that, we know that man is capable of any indignity against His Creator. This is one of the reasons why the Lord Jesus came to earth. How else would the true depths of the nature of man be revealed? It was impossible for man to climb to Heaven to fight against God. If man were to attack God directly, it would have to be by the willingness of God to allow Himself to be attacked. And when the Word was made flesh to dwell among us, that fact immediately revealed what was in man, for hatred was manifested against Christ from the time of His birth—when Herod sought to have Him killed lest there be some danger to his own power. Truly, "the carnal mind is enmity against God" (Rom. 8:7).

And if men are capable of terrible acts against God, is it surprising that they are capable of terrible acts against one another? We have only to read the newspapers to know some of the capacities of men, and anyone who is on the inside will tell you that daily in all our great cities there are crimes committed so terrible, and in such affront to public morality, that even the newspapers exercise a censorship of silence, and the deeds are rarely made public unless a death is involved.

Whatever you do, be sure to apply these truths to yourself. If you draw back in horror and say that you have nothing to do with the terrible state of things described here, you defeat the purpose of the revelation, for God wants to tell you exactly what our state is by nature.

A meadow may be green and fair with wild flowers, and you may think it is all beautiful, but a shepherd guides his sheep away from such fields. He knows that certain flowers indicate the presence of parasites in the soil that will destroy the sheep. And so it is with men. You may appear to be like the green meadow to an observer, but God says the soil of your spirit is, by nature, filled with all the parasites of unrighteousness. These kill any growth Godward, and they can be dealt with only by redemption.

This text in the epistle to the Romans concerning the revelation of the wrath of God from Heaven is one of the few references to judgment that is found in Paul's epistles. Paul was a great preacher of the sovereign grace of God. The word *Hell* is never found in Paul's writings. The doctrine of eternal punishment is singularly the doctrine of the Lord Jesus Christ. Ironically, the One who is often referred to as "the meek and lowly Jesus" is the One who blazed forth most fiercely against the great outbreaks of iniquity. Jesus is the One who announced most firmly that cities and individuals would be brought down to Hell.

Shall not Heaven be purified? Will God not even go to the length of dissolving earth and the Heavens, and creating new Heavens and a new earth in order that righteousness shall be complete and in order that sin may be banished forever? Yes, thank God, He will; and our redeemed hearts rejoice in the love that will pluck out of His kingdom all things that offend and all persons that offend.

One day, several years ago, a man came to me after a meeting and asked me if I believed in Hell. I replied that I certainly did. He pushed the question and asked if I believed in a literal Hell.

I again replied that I believed that Hell was a place to be spelled with a capital initial letter just as much as any city or state should be so spelled. I believe Hell is a place within the boundaries of space, though far off from the small corner of the universe that man has been able to discover with his feeble telescopes.

Finally, the man said to me, "Would you take any animal—I do not ask you if you would take a child—but would you take any animal and put it alive into a fire and see it burn?" I replied that I could conceive of some conditions where I would gladly commit an animal to the flames. If an animal had a horrible disease that could be transmitted to loved ones, I would destroy it without question if I had the opportunity.

We are men and women living in physical bodies that are destructible. We take a murderer and put him in an electric chair or a gas chamber and snuff out his life. We are all responsible for this, for the judge and the executioner are but the agents for the whole of the citizenry. If we deal thus with men who have destructible bodies, how would we deal with them if they were indestructible souls? For that is exactly what men are. Some have attempted to teach that the human soul could have an end, or lose consciousness, but there is no Scripture that can be thus interpreted. And, it is only right that the holiness of God manifests itself in wrath against those who refuse the gift of divine righteousness.

The touchstone of all judgment will be the attitude of men toward the truth of God as set forth in the Word of God. That Word has plainly told us that "the wrath of God is revealed from heaven against all ungodliness and unrighteousness of men, who hold the truth in unrighteousness." We have seen clearly that the natural heart is unrighteous, or not right toward God. But we have also seen that men need not be under God's wrath—on the cross, the Lord Jesus took the full wrath of God upon Him that we might have His mercy and His peace. He took our punishment in order that we prisoners of sin might be set free. Gratitude should move us to take Him at His Word.

> Depth of mercy! can there be
> Mercy still reserved for me?
> Can my God His wrath forbear —
> Me, the chief of sinners, spare?

Thank God, His Word answers, "yes!"

Take Him at His Word. Accept the Savior now. Make Him yours today, that by God's mercy you may never know His wrath.

5

Your Right
To Heaven

We are living in a day when everyone is demanding his or her rights. Labor pleads for the rights of the working man. Industry cries for its rights with equal vigor. Black men demand equal rights with their white brethren. Oriental nations demand independence and national status. And some people are even demanding the right to do as they please regardless of the cost to others.

Among the various rights of men and nations there is one which every man, woman and child must consider—the right to enter Heaven. Have men a right to enter Heaven? This question was anticipated many years ago by the apostle Paul. In language clear, concise, and unequivocal, the great apostle in his letter to the Romans states that no man has any right whatsoever to enter Heaven. In the third chapter of his epistle to the Romans, verses 19 and 20, Paul says, "Now we know that what things soever the law saith, it saith to them who are under the law: that every mouth may be stopped, and all the world may become guilty before God. Therefore by the deeds of the law there shall no flesh be justified in His sight; for by the law is the knowledge of sin." In this passage Paul states that, in the light of man's record and God's perfect standard, *no man has a right to enter Heaven.*

When you first read this you may be shocked and insulted. But look for a moment at the words of the apostle and you will see immediately that there can be no other answer. Let me approach this problem as if you are a patient who has just come to me, a doctor, to find out the state of your health. For just as a doctor has certain diagnostic questions that become almost routine for use with practically every patient, so there are spiritual diagnostic techniques. When a person comes to me with a problem, I follow a definite procedure. First of all, I must find out whether I am dealing with the needs of a believer in Christ or an unbeliever. I ask, "Have you been born again?" If there is an immediate, clear-cut testimony that shows knowledge of redemption and a faith that is committed to Christ as Savior and Lord, the problem itself can be dealt with. But if there is any hesitancy, any wavering, any doubt as to the person's personal salvation, that has to be dealt with first. I say, "Perhaps I can clarify your thinking with a question. You know that there are a great many accidents today. Suppose that you and I should go out of this building and a swerving automobile should come up on the sidewalk and kill the two of us. It is God Himself you must face. And if in this next minute He should say to you, 'What right do you have'—not, 'Why would you like to come,' but—'What right do you have to come into My Heaven?' what would be your answer?"

Literally hundreds of people have had their thinking brought to clarity by following this line of thought. There are three possible answers to this question.

The first answer will be variations on the theme of presenting one's life and works to the scrutiny of God and claiming that he has done the best that he could. Surely, he reasons, God would not be too hard on a sincere man who has plugged along without harming his neighbors too much. The variations are many; a person may boast to have lived always by the Golden Rule, or assert that he has lived up to a certain code. Or, he may insist that he has never been guilty of murder, adultery, and other gross sins.

Two particular conversations will illustrate this tactic to present works to God as the price of entry into Heaven. Early in my ministry I knew a man casually who happened to live a few doors from the church. When I spoke to him about his soul, he laughed me off patronizingly, telling me that he was not the kind of man that needed the church or anything else. He was an active member of a lodge, he said, and if any man lived up to the high principles of that particular lodge, he would be all right.

I saw him from time to time and whenever I attempted to speak to him about his soul he would tell me, once more, that he was living up to his lodge obligations. I am not speaking against lodges here. If you want to drill and exchange passwords and handgrips, and if you want to have an insurance and benevolence scheme with some other men and women, go right ahead. But if you say you can go to Heaven by living up to a society's obligations and principles, you are desperately mistaken.

The sequel of the story will reveal the poverty of any such idea. The day came when this man was stricken with a serious illness and was not expected to live out the day. I went to see him. A member of his lodge was already there on what they called the deathwatch, so that no member of their group would have to die alone. This man was seated across the room from the bed, reading a magazine. I had scarcely entered the room when his successor came, and the "watch" changed, one man leaving and the other man taking his place. The sick man's case was desperate, and a desperate remedy was necessary.

Sitting down by the man's bedside, I said to him, "You do not mind my staying a few minutes and watching you, do you? I have wondered what it would be like to die without Christ. I have known you for several years now as a man who said he did not need Christ but that his lodge obligations were enough. I would like to see a man come to the end that way, to see what it is like."

He looked at me like a wounded animal and slowly said, "You . . . wouldn't . . . mock a . . . dying man . . . would you?" I then asked him what he would answer when God asked him what right he would have to enter the Lord's holy Heaven. Great tears ran down the man's pale and wrinkled cheeks, and he looked at me in agonized silence. Then, swiftly, I told him how he might approach God through the merits of the Lord Jesus Christ. He then began to say that his mother had taught him these things as a child, but that he had abandoned them. But in those moments he came back to God through

Jesus Christ, and in a little while he had the members of his family called that they might hear his testimony of faith. They even heard him say that he wished that his story might be told at his funeral, which it was a few days later.

A second story illustrates the same point from another angle. A young officer of the United States Marines came to visit our church during the war. His brother had become a believer, and the marine was intrigued with the change that had come over his brother. When he was asked if he were saved, he wavered in his reply. Next came the diagnostic question: "What answer would you give if death had just claimed you and God should say to you, 'What right do you have to come into My Heaven?'" He replied that he would say something like, "Well, God, I have never committed any great sins."

"Lieutenant, permit me to be very frank. If you dared attempt any such answer, you could never enter Heaven." He broke in to say, "I have been giving much thought to these things recently, for we have been practicing crawling across a field under live ammunition bursts, and I have wondered what would happen to me if I humped too high." I replied, "Lieutenant, suppose you drive a car up the main street of your city at eighty miles an hour, through all the traffic lights, without any regard to the police whistles. Finally, you are overtaken, and you reach out and slap the policeman. When they finally get you to the court, they throw the book at you. The total of your fine is three hundred dollars. You have no money, but your brother pays your fine for you; and while he is doing it, you start for the door. A policeman says to you, 'What right do you have to leave the court room?' Note the phrase—*what right?* Would you say to him, 'Why, there's my record. I am the man who drove the car up the street at eighty miles an hour and slapped the policeman; so now let me go'?" He answered, "Of course not; I would say that my fine had been paid."

"Exactly! It is not your record that lets you go free; it is your record that brought you there in the first place. And if any man thinks he can arrive in Heaven because of his record, he is not really thinking. It is his record that raises the question. If he had no record with sin in it, he could say, 'Move over, God, and let me sit down on the throne with you. I've arrived at last, and my record brought me in.'" The lieutenant shook his head and said, "Of course, I see it plainly now. It is not my record, but the fact that the Lord Jesus Christ paid my fine by dying on the cross." And thus another man passed out of death and into life.

On another occasion, several years before World War II, we were crossing the Atlantic. It was summer, and I was asked to preach at the Sunday service the second or third day out. After that I had several conversations about spiritual matters with people who came up to ask questions. One conversation was with a young woman who was a professor of languages in one of the Eastern U.S. colleges. I asked the diagnostic question: "If this ship should go to the bottom of the sea, and we were what men called dead, and God asked you: 'What right do you have to come into My Heaven?' what would you say?"

She answered, "I wouldn't have a thing to say." I replied, "You are quoting Paul in Romans 3:19." She was puzzled. I then opened the New Testament to the text (Rom. 3:19) and asked her to read it: "Now we know that what things soever the law saith, it saith to them that are under the law: that every mouth may be stopped, and all the world may become guilty before God." When she had finished, I said, "What does it say? That every mouth may be. . . ." And she read it slowly ". . . stopped. That every mouth may be stopped." "That's right. You said it in modern English—'I wouldn't have a thing to say.' God says that your mouth would be stopped. It is the same thing." And then I led her to see that there is another answer, a great and wonderful answer to the question.

Yes, there are only three possible answers. One: "I'm relying on my record." This is an answer that exists only in present imagination but will never even be uttered when men stand in the clear light of truth "without excuse" (Rom. 1:20). Two: "I wouldn't have a thing to say." That is the horrible truth. You would be speechless as you confronted the Savior who now had become your outraged Judge. The men who pause briefly at the judgment bar of God before going to their eternal doom will never open their lips in their own defense. They will know then that they have no defense, and that they are, indeed, without excuse.

If there is a word spoken at the judgment bar of God by human beings who are being sent to their place in outer darkness, it will be that which is forced from their reluctant lips by an all-powerful God. They will cry, "It was all true, O God. I was wrong. I knew I was wrong when I made my excuses. But I hated and I still hate righteousness by the blood of Christ. I must admit that those despised Christians were right who bowed before Thee and acknowledged their dependence upon Thee. I hated their songs of faith then, and I hate them now. They were right, and I hated them because they were right and because they belonged to Thee, and I hate them now because they belong to Thee. I wanted my own way. And I still want my own way. I want Heaven, but I want Heaven without Thee. I want Heaven with myself on the throne. That's what I want and I do not want anything else and never, never will I want anything other than Heaven with myself on the throne. I want my way. And now I am going to the place of desire without fulfillment, of lust without satisfaction, of wanting without having, of wishing but never getting, of looking but never seeing, and I hate, I hate, I hate because I want my own way. I hate Thee, O God, for not letting me have my way. I hate, I hate. . . ." And their voices will drift off to utter nothingness moaning, "I hate. . . ."

And though there may be such a chorus of the damned, there will never be a word allowed in self defense. They will see truth by the light of truth and will attempt subterfuge no more. Every mouth will be stopped along that line.

Will you sing this chorus of hate? Will you be a member of the chorale of the damned? You need not be. It is true that you can in no wise say that your record gives you the right to enter Heaven. And perhaps you, too, are in the position of the woman who said "I haven't a thing to say," for your mouth is stopped and will be stopped on that great day of judgment. But there is a wonderful third answer to the question, "What right do you have to enter Heaven?" The same apostle that wrote the terrible words which point out to us that our record is not satisfactory to God, also has set forth God's wonderful provision. We read a few verses further on, "Being justified freely by his grace through the redemption that is in Christ Jesus: whom God hath set forth to be a propitiation through faith in his blood, to declare his righteousness for the remission of sins that are past, through the forebearance of God; to declare, I say, at this time his righteousness: that he might be just, and the justifier of him which believeth in Jesus" (Rom. 3:24-26). This is the answer. This gives us the right to enter Heaven.

> Nothing in my hands I bring,
> Simply to Thy cross I cling.
> All for sin could not atone,
> Thou must save and Thou alone.
>
> Rock of ages cleft for me,
> Let me hide myself in Thee.

This is your only plea. This is your only right to enter Heaven. Accept the Lord Jesus Christ as your own personal Savior, and come to know the assurance and peace which He gives.

> The holy, meek, unspotted Lamb,
> Who from the Father's bosom came,
> Who died for me, even me, to atone,
> Now for my Lord, and God, I own.

When from the dust of death I rise
To claim my mansion in the skies,
Even then this shall be all my plea —
Jesus hath lived, hath died for me!

Ah! give to all Thy servants, Lord,
With power to speak Thy gracious Word,
That all who to Thy wounds will flee,
May find eternal life in Thee.

6
What Is
Salvation?

The word that is used in the original language for *salvation* covers the entire work of God on behalf of the human soul. No one, not even if he has spent much time in the study of the Word of God, can fully comprehend the height and the depth of the vast subject of salvation. (The depth is our need; the height is the provision that God has made.) Salvation begins when the sinner recognizes the fact that he is less perfect than God and therefore under condemnation. God comes to you today, just as you are. There is nothing that you have to do in order to draw His attention to you. You do not have to make yourself better in order for Him to start His work. There is an old hymn that puts it well:

> Let not conscience make you linger,
> Nor of fitness fondly dream.
> All the fitness He requireth
> Is to feel your need of Him.

God comes to you regardless of your education or the lack of it. He comes to you regardless of your prejudices, or how they were formed. He comes to you with the declaration that you are in a position that is desperate without His help, but He tells you that He is ready to furnish the help you need.

Unfortunately, some turn away from Him because they live in a world where illusions are so plentiful. It is easy to think that since you are getting along well in the world that you are also getting along well in your relationship with God. The fact is that you are lying in the embrace of death and do not realize your need.

A Chinese evangelist was once preaching on the street in a town in China. He spoke of the weight of sin and a heckler called out to ask how much that weight was. Fifty pounds? A hundred pounds? The evangelist answered: "A corpse lying in his coffin will not feel a hundred pound weight on his chest any more than a fifty pound weight." So the weight of sin is upon the human soul, and it is only when the Holy Spirit makes us conscious of need that we can feel the weight of sin and turn to the Savior who is able to lift it.

If you think that you have any ability or virtue that can help you gain entrance to Heaven, you do not understand your own nature or the magnitude of the task which is demanded of you. A man might be the world champion Olympic swimmer, but if he were suddenly thrown overboard in the midst of the ocean, reaching the shore would be totally beyond his powers. And God declares that you are overboard in the sea of sin that estranges you from Him. No breast-stroke of emotion can bring you to the shore. You must recognize your lost position and submit yourself to His sovereign grace.

God commands men everywhere to repent. Repentance does not mean an emotional state, "being sorry" for your sins. It is derived from a Greek expression for the military command of "Right about face." You have been facing yourself, trusting in your own ability while Christ has been behind you, despised and rejected by you. You must about face. You must despise and reject your own efforts for salvation. You must realize that God has done all the work through the Savior and that He requires you to put your trust in Him.

The gospel of Jesus Christ is the power of God unto salvation from sin's penalty. "For the wages of sin is death; but the gift of God is eternal life through Jesus Christ our Lord" (Rom. 6:23). The soul is separated from God by sin and will remain separated forever if not restored by the grace of God.

This is the first work of salvation and that which we hear about most frequently. It is the proclamation to man that he is in death and darkness and that he will remain there for the unending ages if he is not saved from the penalty of sin. The penalty of sin is that the unbeliever walks in darkness. The penalty of walking in darkness is to be cast eternally into outer darkness. When you are saved, the penalty of your sin has been remitted, and your fine has been paid so that you may be restored to fellowship with our holy God.

Reduced to its most elemental concept, we can say that Christianity is expressed in the following propositions: I deserve Hell; Jesus Christ took my Hell; there is nothing left for me but His Heaven. There is the great fact of past-tense salvation for the Christian. Christ *paid* sin's penalty. When one has been born again he knows that this salvation, his present possession, is something that has been finished forever.

But salvation is also in the present tense. We are being saved from the power of sin. This does not mean that the Christian never has any further outbreak of sin. But it does mean that a power has been provided for us which enables us to live with sin beneath us. When the Lord Jesus was born, the angel said, "Thou shalt call his name JESUS: for he shall save his people from their sins" (Matt. 1:21).

If we are to understand this phase of salvation, it is necessary for us to realize that there is a great deal of difference between sin and sins. *Sin* may be compared to poison in the bloodstream and *sins* compared to the breaking out of the boil on the surface of the body. Both of these must be dealt with. When we are first saved, (which we have called "salvation in the past tense") God deals with *sin,* the poison. (Of course, the illustration cannot be pushed to extremes, for the old nature of sin is not removed. Because of this there is the day-by-day warfare in connection with our salvation from the power of sin.) However, the promise is there, "Sin shall not have dominion over you: for you are not under the law, but under grace" (Rom. 6:14).

Some men attempt to deal with *sins* before they deal with *sin.* Any attempt at moral reform apart from salvation through the blood of Jesus Christ is like putting salve on a surface sore instead of dealing with the poison in the bloodstream. In this way, it is possible to drive the sore to another part of the body. The boil goes from the neck to the back or from the nose to the lip. Society takes the attitude that the presence of boils cannot be helped but they must be kept out of sight. It is only the indiscretion of sin that goes beyond the bounds of propriety (and lands a man in prison or in the asylum or in the hospital) which is considered bad taste. All that is done discreetly is acceptable to society. Sin in silk is not frowned upon, although sin in rags is distinctly not proper etiquette.

The gospel of Jesus Christ is also the power of God unto salvation in the future tense. It would be a sorry gospel indeed if our hope were in this life alone. If such were the case, we would be, as Paul writes to the Corinthians, "of all men most miserable" (I Cor. 15:19). Are we doomed to see our bodies degenerate and our mental powers decline? Are we doomed to come to the end of all things in a narrow grave with a slab of marble weighing us down? Thank God the death of the believer is but his entrance into glory. Peter writes a great paragraph concerning that which is in store for the believers. "Blessed be the God and Father of our Lord Jesus Christ, who according to his abundant mercy hath begotten us again unto a lively hope by the resurrection of Jesus Christ from the dead, to an inheritance incorruptible and undefiled, and that fadeth not away, reserved in heaven for you, who are kept by the power of God through faith unto salvation ready to be revealed in the last time" (I Peter 1:3-5).

This tremendous, three-fold salvation is for every one who believes. Do not think for one moment that it is possible to be saved without faith. This raises some definite questions about the nature of faith and about our object of faith.

Faith is belief, and no matter by which name you call it, it is simply acting upon the word of another. If you wish to go from New York to Chicago, you pick up the telephone and call the railroad station or airport. You ask for the hour of departure of trains or planes going to Chicago. The clerk tells you the time of the train and you pack your bag and go down to the station a few minutes before the hour that was given you. You buy your ticket and normally the train will be ready to leave and will pull out on time. You have acted upon the word that was spoken to you by someone you had never seen in your life. That is faith. And in the realm of spiritual things faith is simply acting upon the Word of God. He tells you that he put your sin on Christ and crucified Him in your place. He tells you that He raised the Lord Jesus Christ from the dead as a sign that by Him all who believe are justified from all things. God produces a supernatural result when we rest completely in His Word about the work that was done for us.

The wages of sin is death, but the gift of God is eternal life through Jesus Christ our Lord. Every man as a sinner must collect these death wages if he does not receive God's gift. The Lord Jesus Christ died on the cross for every man. He died for you. Will you not take God at His Word and act upon it? Will you not accept His Son as your Savior?

7

Can You
Be Bought?

"Can I be bought?" What a question! It would appear as though I were insulting you, because the use of the expression, "Can you be bought?" generally means, "Will you accept a bribe?" And the expression, "To be bought" has become an expression of opprobrium. But in the present day in which we live bribery seems to be the common practice, although the many manifestations of this act are not called by this term.

However, I am not asking this question in these terms. I am asking it in terms of the Word of God. In Peter's first epistle, chapter 1, verses 18 and 19, we read, "Ye know that ye were not redeemed with corruptible things, as silver and gold, from your vain conversation received by tradition from your fathers; but with the precious blood of Christ, as of a lamb without blemish and without spot." These are great words, because they tell us that God has found a way whereby He can buy or redeem man. A redemption has been made necessary because of man's sin. We read in the Scriptures that all have sinned and come short of the glory of God.

We need not argue whether man is a sinner or not. The very evidence of his life proves that he is. Isaiah, the prophet of old, gives a great demonstration of this when he says, "But the wicked are like the troubled sea, when it cannot rest, whose waters cast up mire and dirt. There is no peace, saith my God, to the wicked" (Isa. 57:20). Men are afraid to die. Realizing that they must some day face a just and holy God, their lives fulfill the testimony of the Scriptures: "Forasmuch then as the children are partakers of flesh and blood, he also himself likewise took part of the same; that through death he might destroy him who has the power of death, that is, the devil; and deliver them who through fear of death were all their lifetime subject to bondage" (Heb. 2:14, 15). The restlessness of the human spirit and the fear of the afterlife are two great proofs that men are sinners, facing judgment without a Savior.

God's desire is not to condemn men but to save them from this judgment. He Himself warned men: "The soul that sinneth it shall die." And, "The wages of sin is death." But He also said: "For God so loved the world that He gave His only begotten Son, that whosoever believeth on Him should not perish but have everlasting life" (John 3:16). If there is one thing the gospel reveals, it is man's complete ruin in sin and God's perfect remedy in Christ. The remedy we speak of has a theological term, namely, justification. To justify is to make man right with God, to make him acceptable to God, to bring him back, as it were, on the level with God. And this must be done at a price—the price of redemption. Man must be bought by the blood of Christ.

Let us be quite clear as to the meaning of the word "justify" before we proceed to the basis and method of its communication to us. To justify is to regard as righteous. It includes the removal of man's guilt as well as his condemnation. This is the great difference between a human tribunal and the divine judgment. A king can give his royal clemency or pardon, but he cannot reinstate the criminal to the position of one who has not broken the law. God does both, and this is the meaning of justification. Pardon concerns the past only, and cannot possibly deal with a man's future relation to the law; but God deals with both, and the two together define justification.

The basis of our justification is redemption. The prefix "re" in *redeem* means "again" (as in *re*copy, *re*wash, *re*write). The main part of the word is from a root that means "to purchase, to buy." So an article that is left in a pawn shop can be redeemed by paying the money that was borrowed, plus the interest charges. The word is also used when a company finds it possible to call some of its indebtedness, pay the borrower, and cancel the obligation: this is the *redemption* of bond issues.

In the Bible, the word also covers the idea of deliverance by the payment of a price. The English word "redeem" translates three different Greek words, each of which has a rich meaning in connection with our salvation. One Greek word, *apolutro*, means "to loose, untie, deliver." This idea is to be found in the first chapter of Revelation where a psalm is sung "unto him who loved us, and loosed us from our sins through his own blood" (Rev. 1:5). Thayer says of this verb, "Everywhere in the New Testament this word is used to denote deliverance effected through the death of Christ from the retributive wrath of a holy God and the merited penalty of sin."

Another Greek word used in the Scriptures and translated by our word "redemption" is *agorazo*, the common Greek word for marketing. The noun *agora* means the market place, and the verb *agorazo* means to buy. In the New Testament the word is applied to the purchase of souls. This would be readily understood in the ancient world, since there was a slave market that operated almost every day, and the traffic in slaves was very great. That Christ should have walked into the slave market and purchased, or redeemed, men who were slaves of sin, would have been easily comprehended.

This idea is further clarified by the fact that the Bible speaks of the price of our redemption in the verse we have already seen, "Ye were . . . redeemed . . . with the precious blood of Christ, as of a lamb without blemish and without spot" (I Peter 1:18, 19). Thus we sing:

Nor silver, nor gold hath obtained my
   redemption,
No riches of earth could have saved my
   poor soul;
The blood of the cross is my only
   foundation,
The death of my Saviour now maketh
   me whole.
I am redeemed, but not with silver,
I am bought, but not with gold;
Bought with a price, the blood of Jesus,
Precious price of love untold.

Again, there is another very beautiful sidelight on this truth of our redemption by purchase in the market place to be found in another phrase of the New Testament. In Peter's epistle, Christians are called "a peculiar people." The English word *peculiar* has changed in its meaning until now it indicates that there is something queer, strange, or erratic about the person who is called peculiar. This is unfortunate. *Peculiar* is derived from the Latin word for cattle. In Roman days, there was no such thing as money as we know it in coin or paper. Almost everything was priced in cows, in the same way that many articles are priced in goats in parts of Africa today. If a thing in the Latin world had a high value, it was worth a lot of cows—the word is *pecus*—and therefore, it had a cow value, a pecuniary value. And an article which was rare and valuable was peculiar, worth a great price.

When the Bible tells us that Christians are a peculiar people, it means that we are a people redeemed at a great price, and that our redemption cost the death of the Lord Jesus Christ and the shedding of His blood. The very same Greek words translated "peculiar people" in Peter's epistle are translated "purchased possession" in Ephesians, which describes believers as the objects of the redemptive work of Christ, and as the center of His work.

There is another Greek word (similar to the one we first considered) which gives additional light on the thought of redemption. The word is *exagorazo, (agorazo* with the prefix *ex)* and carries the idea of buying something *out* of the market. There is a difference between a purchase that is for resale and a purchase that is made in order to take an article out of commerce. For example, a dealer in rare books and works of art might purchase an item at a London or New York sale, and hold it for resale to a customer. Some pictures, books, manuscripts, and other art objects are bought and sold again and again. But finally, when a great work of art is bought by a museum, it is thus taken out of circulation permanently. An example of this is a Shakespeare folio which was bought and sold in several sales until it came to rest in the Folger Shakespeare Library in Washington, D. C. Under the terms of the trust it is to remain there permanently, and can never be put into the market again.

The Greek word *exagorazo* carries this connotation. When the Lord Jesus Christ stepped into the slave market and paid the ransom for guilty sinners, it was a price paid once for all. It can never be repeated. On the cross He cried out, "It is finished" (John 19:30). The Lord bought us in order that He might take us out of the market of sin. It is possible, then, for us to say with Paul, "I am persuaded, that neither death, nor life, nor angels, nor principalities, nor powers, nor things present, nor things to come, nor height, nor depth, nor any other creature, shall be able to separate us from the love of God, which is in Christ Jesus our Lord" (Rom. 8:38, 39).

One of the most beautiful illustrations in the Bible sets forth this truth. Hosea, the preacher, was married to a harlot, and he kept loving her, even when she ran away from him and sank to the utmost degradation. Eventually she was reduced to slavery, and was brought to the auction block to be sold to the highest bidder. This story is in the third chapter of Hosea: "And the

Lord said to me, 'Go again, love a woman who is beloved of a paramour and is an adulteress; even as the Lord loves the people of Israel, though they turn to other gods . . .'" (RSV). Hear God telling the preacher to act out of love. We read: "Love her as the Lord loves the people of Israel." *Now* I know how God loves, when I see Christ dying to redeem me. *Now* I can comprehend the love of God, when I see Him coming into the slave market and laying down the price of His blood to purchase me and take me out of the market forever.

The next verse tells the story. "So I bought her for fifteen pieces of silver, and for a bushel and a half of barley." Now the husband has become her owner. Before this moment, if Hosea had harmed his wife, he would have been accountable with his life. But now that he has bought and paid for her, she is his as a chattel to do with as he wishes. So what does he do? Listen to the words of love as he puts her veil back on her face and shields her from the gaze of Jerusalem. We read, "And I said unto her, thou shalt abide for me many days; thou shalt not play the harlot, and thou shalt not be for another man." The husband bought her in order that she might be faithful to him. And then comes the culmination of it all, as the husband says to the wife whom he has purchased, "So will I also be for thee."

There is no greater love then this. The Lord Jesus redeemed us. We are His purchased possession. He paid Himself for us that He might have us to dwell in, that He might be formed within us, and revealed through us, so that men might glorify and praise Him for His love, and grace, and mercy.

When we put all three of the words for redemption together, we discover that our Lord went down into the slave market where we were exposed to the gaze of the universe as slaves of sin—lost, dead, and under the curse of God. He bought us with the price of His own life in order that He might take us out of the marketplace forever. He did this so that we might be forever delivered from sin and sins, and so that we might be to the praise of the glory of His grace, exhibits of His eternal love.

It is true that when we were yet sinners Christ died for the ungodly. It is true that we were declared righteous when we were still in our sin, but the purpose of all of this is our holiness. There can be no true comprehension of redemption apart from the fact that He bought us to set us free from sins in order that we might become the servants of righteousness. The deliverance includes freedom from the guilt or penalty of sin, from the mastery or power of sin in our daily lives and, ultimately, our deliverance from even the presence of sin.

An Englishman has written a paragraph that describes the compelling, constraining movement to holiness that is the result of redemption through Christ. He writes: "When I discover that I am forgiven I shall condemn my sin more sternly than ever. I see that it was inexcusable. I abhor it as never before; I may feel as I have never felt, that it justly provoked the divine indignation and wrath; but when I approach God through Christ as the propitiation for my sin, the guilt of it crushes me no longer; God is

66

at peace with me; I have perfect rest in His love. It is not merely at the commencement of the Christian life that the death of Christ has this wonderful power. Its power endures. Day after day, year after year, when we are troubled by the consciousness of moral failure, we find in the death of Christ for our sin, power to trust in the divine mercy, and to implore the divine forgiveness with an absolute confidence that we shall receive it."

8
The Christian Walk

There is something stately and beautiful about a walk which we in this age of cars and airplanes are in danger of losing. In my student days I took a long walking trip in France. It was not for a morning or an afternoon, but it was for the entire month of June. I set off through the countryside; the forest of Fontainebleau, the little village of Mure-sur-Loing, Sens and its old cathedral (prototype of Canterbury), the smiling villages of Burgundy and its old houses, and then the pine-filled hills of Jura, the lake of Geneva, and the Alps beyond.

There is something indescribable and incomparable about a walking trip. The sight of an old village upon a far hill when you approach it one step at a time cannot quite be put into words. I do not know how many times since then I have stood—a continent and an ocean away from those scenes—and breathed once more the air of that countryside.

The way a man walks reveals his character. The words which have been used to describe various ways of walking bring such different pictures to our minds that we realize that the way we walk reveals our attitudes and even our character. A slouch, a shuffle, a brisk walk, smart step, a prowl, hesitating steps, lagging gait—all these describe more than just ways men walk.

It is not surprising, therefore, to find in the Bible the life of a Christian described under the figure of a "walk." We wish to consider the walk of the Christian from four different points of view. To Abram, God said, "I am the Almighty God, walk *before* me. . ." (Gen. 17:1). Through Moses God commanded the children of Israel, "Ye shall walk *after* the Lord your God. . ." (Deut. 13:4). Of two of the patriarchs, Enoch and Noah, it is written that they walked *with* God (Gen. 5:24; 6:9). Finally, in the New Testament we find it written, "As ye have therefore received Christ Jesus the Lord, so walk ye *in* him" (Col. 2:6). We are told, then, to walk *before* the Lord, *after* the Lord, *with* the Lord, and *in* the Lord. Let us examine the significance of these phases of our Christian life; the truths revealed are beautiful.

However, before considering these four phases let me make it quite plain that no one can walk unless he is on his feet, and no one can walk the Christian life until he has turned from self and placed his faith in Christ.

For the Christian, the possessor of the life of Christ, we now consider the growth of that life as our Christian walk. First, we are told to walk *before* the Lord. This gives us a picture of childhood. Many of us can remember, perhaps, incidents of our own childhood when we walked before our own parents. I can recall our Sunday morning walk to Sunday school. I would skip along the sidewalk, stopping to examine a place in the cement where a group of children had left the prints of their hands and bare feet when it was wet, and where a horseshoe had been imbedded in the walk. There was a certain place where I would run far ahead and wait at the curb for my father to come up, that I might cross with him. There was one yard before which I paused, waiting for my father to come up close, that I might have him near me as I passed a huge, barking dog. Walking *before* my father, I was in a place of absolute safety. His eye was ever upon me, and his voice could call out if I strayed from the way he wanted me to go.

Certainly it is so with our Heavenly Father. He has us walk before Him in the path of great security. "He knoweth the way that I take" (Job 23:10). We need never fear when our Heavenly Father is behind us. He started us on this walk, and put us there in His sight, and He expects to bring us home. Jeremiah heard the Lord say, "For I know the thoughts that I think toward you, saith the Lord, thoughts of peace, and not of evil, to give you an expected end" (Jer. 29:11). And surely, this is in the heart of the Father.

But walking before the Father also speaks of training and discipline. I can see a father and his children who took their walk day by day, in the midst of the big city where they lived. There were perils of traffic, and other city dangers, on every hand. The training went on, day by day. The children walked before their father and were told that they might run ahead to a certain tree, some fifty yards away. I can see them running up to the fixed goal and standing with their toes to a line; little soldiers obeying with absolute precision.

Then when they had been trained so well that they never over-shot their prescribed limit, the distance was raised. Finally they were released at a certain point and told that they could go ahead, disappear out of sight around the corner, and stop at a certain known goal. When that lesson had been learned, they ultimately were permitted to cross a quiet street where there was little danger of traffic. Where three-year-old steps had been halted at fifty yards, and four-year-old steps had been permitted to go around a corner and out of sight, five-year-old steps were crossing streets.

This is why the Heavenly Father tells His children to walk before Him. He desires their growth, their discipline, their training, that they may be strong in the powers that He has given them.

In the second place, we are told that we are to walk *after* the Lord. This teaches us the great truth of precept, example, and following. We learn to be followers of our God, shaping our lives by His blessed example. Let not the non-Christian think that he can walk in the path of the Lord. As we have pointed out, the non-Christian is dead in trespasses and sins. Only the believer can look to the Lord's life as the example of his walk. "Christ . . . suffered for us, leaving us an example, that [we] should follow his steps" (I Peter 2:21).

Clearly we are taught that following "the steps of Christ" is following His sufferings. The world hated Him; the world will always hate the true believer. Christ gave the clear outline of what following Him would really mean: "If the world hate you," He said, "ye know that it

72

hated me before it hated you. If ye were of the world, the world would love his own: but because ye are not of the world, but I have chosen you out of the world, therefore the world hateth you. Remember the word that I said unto you, The servant is not greater than his lord" (John 15:18-20).

Walking *after* the Lord is the true explanation of what it means to take up our cross and follow Him. Too often there is a total misconception of what a cross means for a Christian. For example, a mother once told me that she had a very heavy cross to bear; her son was in prison. That was not a cross; that was a personal tragedy, a tragedy of sin. Another woman said that her cross was a cancer. That was not a cross; that was disease, the common lot of humanity.

The only cross in the Bible is the cross of Jesus Christ. When the believer is told that he is to deny self, to take up his cross daily, and to follow Christ (Luke 9:23), he is being instructed that he must count himself as being crucified with Christ, that his old nature should be yielded over for crucifixion death, and that in taking up the cross he is taking up likeness to Christ's sufferings, "who, when he was reviled, reviled not again; when he suffered, he threatened not; but committed himself to him that judgeth righteously (I Pet. 2:23). It is to this life that we are called, and it is specifically stated that this is Christ's example, and we are to follow His steps.

But with all of the sufferings of the Christian life there are pre-eminent compensations. If we walk *before* the Lord to learn, and if we follow *after* Him in His sufferings, there is also the

73

privilege of walking *with* Him, in fruitful companionship. Friends walk together. Two cannot walk together unless they are agreed (Amos 3:3 and II Cor. 6:14). When we are told that we are to walk with our Lord, it is understood that we shall have put down our wills in order that we might fully accept His will.

Walking *with* God is fellowship and companionship, but it is also surrender to His will and attributes, and agreement with Him. The man who follows Christ accepts the holiness of the Lord as the supreme standard of living and accepts the sovereignty of God as the final court of right in words and deeds. There could be no fellowship apart from the clear recognition of the Lord's wisdom and knowledge—which overrules all of man's and Satan's devices—and of the Lord's authority in the believer's own life, to will and to do of His good pleasure (Phil. 2:13). The man who walks with God will know Him as Lord and Master, will know Him as sovereign in history and circumstance, and will be permeated with His very spirit of judgment.

And finally, we are told that "as ye have therefore received Christ Jesus the Lord, so walk ye in him." This is the climax of all our walking. To walk in Christ is to recognize the richness of our position in Him, and to see our lives as being hid with Christ in God (Col. 3:3). The little word "in" is one of the most potent in the New Testament. If the epistles are read with care, it will be discovered that this little preposition appears coupled with a name of Christ or a pronoun of that name in scores of instances. "If any man be *in* Christ, he is a new creation" (II Cor. 5:17); we are "accepted *in* the beloved" (Eph.

74

1:6); "*in* whom we have redemption through his blood" (Eph. 1:7); and we are "blessed with all spiritual blessings in heavenly places *in* Christ" (Eph. 1:3). These are many other passages identify the position of the believer with Christ.

We recognize that our salvation is secure to us because God looked upon us as being *in* Christ when our Lord suffered upon the cross. We are aware that God calls us to holy living—because He counts us as having been quickened with Christ when He was raised from the dead (Col. 3:1; Eph. 2:5). We see the great truth of our ascension with Him, that we are counted as being already seated in the Heavens with Christ (Eph. 2:6). All of these phases of truth are summed up in the obligation that is upon us because of our glorious position "in" Christ.

We have been trained to walk before Him; we are called to look upon His sufferings and to be willing to walk after Him. He takes us into His closest fellowship and bids us walk with Him. All of this obliges us to bring every thought and action into subjection to Christ. Every phase of our life is to be lived within the position that is ours by His death, resurrection, and ascension. We are in Christ. We have received all this by grace. So let us walk in Him, glorifying Him in our body and in our spirit, which are God's (I Cor. 6:20).

May the Lord give us grace, day by day, to walk *before* Him, *after* Him, *with* Him, and *in* Him.